To the memory
of my mother,
Lucy Walter

Woody and Me

by Mary Neville

PICTURES BY RONNI SOLBERT

PANTHEON BOOKS

List of Poems

Woody and Me

Pleasant Street

In our town there's a street
Called Pleasant Street.
We don't live on it.
At breakfast, if Woody and me
Are arguing,
Mother says,
"Well—
They wouldn't let *us*
Live on Pleasant Street."

Tempers

Boy, when Woody's mad
He can really *roar*.
I don't know, but I suppose
They hear *me* through the door,
Too.

Art

Why do some people
Ask you
What it is?
Sometimes
Woody and I
Just like to paint
Nothin'.

Complaining Day

I was complaining
Today.
I thought of all the
Bad Things:

    Make my bed.
    Carry out garbage.
    Go to bed earlier than
    Other kids.
    Can't watch T.V. on
    School nights.

But I remembered some
Good Things:

    Woody,
    Mother and Dad,
    Not sick much,
    Not dead,
    My bike,
    Saturday.

That is quite a
Lot
Of good ones.

The Squad Car

Woody had a birthday party,
Without any girls.
He got seven guns
From seven boys,
And a Dick Tracy Detective Squad Car
From me.

He loved the guns.
But most of all
He loved the squad car,
With mean-looking detectives
Painted on,
Looking out the windows
For robbers,
And a siren,
A flashing spotlight,
And a wind-up key.

The seven boys and
Woody and me
Wound and wound and wound that key.

We pulled down all the shades.
That squad car
Went circling around
Flashing its spotlight,
Screaming its siren,
Like a real car
Going to a robbery
About ninety miles an hour!

Then
Somehow
The key got knocked
Down
A hole in the wall,
Where Daddy was
Fixing the wiring.

Oh
How we fished
For that key!
The seven boys and
Woody and me.

But it was
Down
Inside the wall.

Mother wrote a letter
To the toy company
For a new key.

They never answered.

Mother tied a magnet
To a string
And let it down
The hole in the wall.
The magnet came up
With three safety pins
And a paper clip.

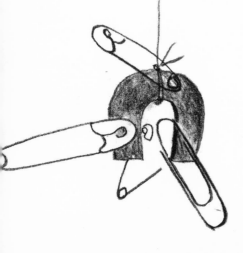

Daddy tried pliers
And things
In the keyhole,
But the squad car
Just sat.

A neighbor loaned us
An old-fashioned clock key,
But it didn't fit our squad car.

Nearly one year passed.

The seven guns were
All broken and in pieces,
But the squad car on a shelf
Was as shiny and bright
As the day it was made.

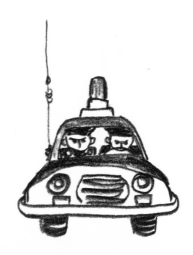

The Last Part of the Squad Car Story

It was nearly
Woody's next birthday.
Then
Mother had an
Idea.

Why don't we get Woody
Another squad car?
Then he'll have
Two cars,
And
A key!

It was a secret
Between Mother and
Dad and
Me.

Can you guess?

The Dick Tracy Detective Squad Car,
That year's model,
Had the key
WELDED INTO
The keyhole.

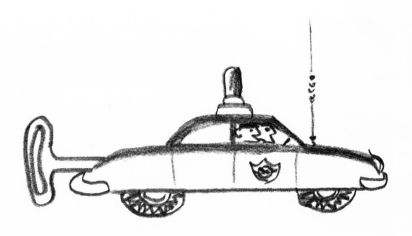

Daddy said
That toy company
Must have gotten
A hundred thousand letters
About lost keys.
No wonder
They never answered.

Woody had this
Next birthday party,
Without any girls.
He got a lot of guns
From a lot of boys,
And the *new* squad car
From me.

He said I could have
The old squad car.
I used to push it around
A little
Sometimes.

One day
I made a new friend.
On his toy shelf in a box
Of rubber bands and old
Cracker Jack prizes,
I saw
A Dick Tracy squad car key!
"I used to have
A squad car," he said.
"But it got wrecked."

I traded him three marbles
For
The key!

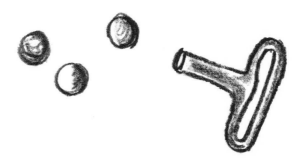

Mother and Dad and
Woody and
Me
Wound and wound and wound
That key!

Boy.
Do TWO squad cars
Make a lot of noise!

Sucking Sap

In the cold spring
Our maple tree
Had long icicles of sap
Hanging from the tips
Of the branches.
Golly, they were good to eat.
At first I thought
They tasted just like water.
But when I saw
All the kids eating them,
I knew they tasted awfully sweet.

Christmas Pageant

Our class is practicing
And practicing
To spell out
The M-E-R-R-Y part of
MERRY CHRISTMAS.

Chuckie is a big M.
He says,
"M is for the Many toys—"
Joannie is a big E.
I forget what she says.
I am a *space*.
I *wait* a minute.

It Takes All Kinds

We know some kids
Who said, "No thank you,"
When Dad asked them
To have some candy.
Very nice kids, too.
Some things are hard
To figure out.
Weren't they hungry?
Didn't they like candy?
Or what?

Social Studies

Woody says, "Let's *make* our soap.
It's easy.
We learned about it
In school."
He told Mother,
"All you do is
Take a barrel.
Bore holes in the sides,
And fill it with straw.
Ashes on top—"

"No," said Mother.

The Morning That Seemed
Like Forever

At eight-thirty
All the kids
Crushed up the stairs and
Into school.

George put his
Jacket on
My hook.
So
I put my jacket on
His hook.
This started an
Argument.

School was the
Same.
After arithmetic
Came
Spelling.
And after spelling
There was
Social studies.

Outside the window
I saw the gym boys
Running past in their
White underwear.

The heater blower
Went on,
And the furnace pipes
Rattled
  Down
    Below.

The school secretary
Came in
To get the
New girl for
Eye and ear
Testing

I remembered
Breakfast,
Far away.

The thirty-four
Children, the teacher,
And I
Had been
In the room about
A year
Since
Eight-thirty.

A bell rang!

I took my
Jacket off
George's hook,
And went out
The door.

I kicked
A can halfway
Home.
Then I lost it
In the street.

I hollered
Very LOUD, and
Listened to myself.
"School Is Over."

I ran in the house
And up the stairs.
"School Is Over," I
Hollered at Mother.

"Why, Johnny," she said,
"This is only lunch!
You have half a day
Left."

OH, NO!

Remembering

Dad said,
"Remember your manners."

At school the teacher
Tells you to remember,
Remember.

I *am* trying.

But I have so *many*
Things
To remember.
I have to remember
The names
Of *thirty-four*
Children.

Changing Places

The Principal said,
"Try to
Put yourself
In my place,
Next time."

I tried.
But I just
Couldn't.

Three Minutes

Woody was practicing for
His Oral Book Report.
It had to be
Just
Three minutes,
The teacher
Said.

"That sure isn't
Very much time,"
Woody said.
"I'll have to leave
Out half the book."

But I suppose that
Three minutes of someone
Talking
Can seem very
Continuous.

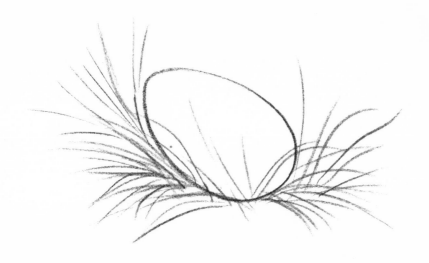

The Enormous Easter Egg Hunt

Every year
The big kids win
The Grand Prize
In our town's egg hunt.
They always find the Golden Egg.

This year
Woody had a plan.
He and Willie
Were going to get up
Real early.
Go down to the park
Before the hunt began.
Find the Golden Egg.
Then go back
When the hunt began.
Get it.
And collect the
Grand Prize.

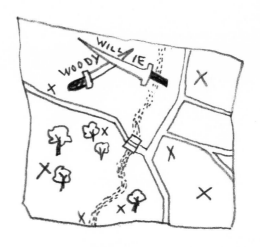

I got the paper and pencil
For Woody
To draw
The plan.
He put in
A lot of streets, the bridge,
The river, the park,
And lots of X's stuck in
Here and there.
He drew two crossed daggers
At the top,
One marked Willie,
One marked Woody.

He and Willie were going to
Hide
Behind this bush marked X,
In case anyone
Might be following.
"But Woody," I said,
"What if the
Big kids
See you!"

"How *can* they see us
When
We're zigzagging
In and out of the bushes?
When the hunt starts,
We'll *come* back,
Get the Golden Egg,
And *collect* the Prize!"

The morning of
The Enormous Easter Egg Hunt
We looked out the window.
We couldn't tell
Whether it was raining softly
Or just looked like
It was going to rain softly.

"I think it's going
To be awful squshy
Down there in the park,"
I said.

Woody phoned
Willie,
And Willie said he had to
Go get his hair cut.

Mother drove me and
Woody
Down to the hunt about eleven.
There were a thousand kids
Looking for a thousand eggs.

I found one purple egg
And Woody found
One pink egg
That someone had
Stepped on.

Someday
Woody and I
Are going to a *real*
Enormous Egg Hunt,
In a green park,
With a hundred thousand
Eggs
Lying all over everything.

Being
George

Woody and I
Call each other "George,"
Sometimes.
When we're playing truck,
Or something like that.
If you call yourself "George,"
It makes you feel
Pretty grown up.
(If you're a little boy
Whose name is *really*
George,
You'd have to think up
A different name.
Maybe "Herb.")

People Named Bill

Some very nice people
Are named Bill.
A little Bill is
My best friend.
Another Bill—
A middle one—
Has a clubhouse
With a flag on top.
A big Bill
Works at our store,
And lets me
Have old orange crates.

Discovery

Woody called me
To come quick.
He was looking down
At a little pile of dirt.
Woody's face was happy.
"I think I've discovered
A new kind
Of bug
In the world!"
He said.

I never had seen
One
Of them before,
Either.

Darkness

Woody and I shut
Our eyes and
Groped around
The living room,
Bumping into
Tables and chairs.

We wouldn't let
Ourselves
Open our eyes,
For a while.

A person
Who is really
Blind
Never opens
His eyes.

Choices

If I had to choose,
Would I rather have
Day
All the time,
Or
Night?

No stars?
I wouldn't like
That.

No sun?
I'd always be
Wanting
It.

I'll take
Stars and
Sun,
The way
It is.

Tearing Around

Woody and I just like
To go tearing around
Sometimes.
Hollering too.

Inside or outside will do.
But Mother
Would rather
It was outside.

The Man Who Was Never Jolly

Some people are jolly,
And some are not.
Woody and I like
The jolly kind.
Our mailman is the
Not-jolly kind.
He never says a word.
When it rains,
He comes under
The most enormous
Black umbrella
I have ever seen.
Once he talked to Mother.
He said,
"If you don't keep
Your dog inside,
I won't bring you
The mail."

Iodine

I can make myself
Be quiet
When iodine is put on.
But it's easier
For me
To yell quite loud.

People Named Bill Are Lucky for Me

This is going to be a sad story
At first.
But then it gets happy.

It's about kids and their friends.

Once I didn't have one kid
To play with.

It's hard to explain
When you don't know yourself.
Mario and I played rockets together,
And guns,
And watched T.V.,
And ate popcorn.

Then Mario got a new friend.
I didn't even know his name.
He and Mario wouldn't
Play with me any more.

I could still play rockets,
And guns,
And watch T.V.,
And eat popcorn,
By myself.

It gets very boring
When those big T.V. ladies
Are selling
Things,
And you're the only one
Looking.

Woody said,
"You'll be O.K."
But I didn't believe him.

Then one day
The big Bill who saves
Old orange crates
For me
Said,
"Here's another kid
Is building a fort."

This new kid and I
Put our boxes together.
This little Bill had
Shiny eyes.
We built
Our fort up very tall.

It's funny
How people named Bill
Are lucky for me.

And Woody
Was right.

Lemons and Apples

One day I might feel
Mean,
And squinched up inside,
Like a mouth sucking on a
Lemon.

The next day I could
Feel
Whole and happy
And right,
Like an unbitten apple.

Business

Woody says
It's easy
To make money.

In half an hour
At his juice stand,
He made
Thirty-seven cents.

Night Lights

At night when I go to bed,
I like to have a light—
Just a small one—
Like in the closet.
The dark is nice,
But so is a light.
Woody says he doesn't care,
But he's fond
Of the light on the stair.
So he leaves his door
Open.

Candy or Canary?

Some people like children.
They keep candy
To give if children come to call.
Some people don't keep candy.
Often they prefer dogs,
Or canary birds instead.
You can tell pretty quickly.

Evening

We like a
Sky
That looks like
Flocks of sheep,
All going home,
Maybe about five o'clock
In the evening,
When Woody and me
Are going home
Too.